OnBoard
ACADEMICS

I0220709

Sentences

© 2015 OnBoard Academics, Inc
Portsmouth, NH
800-596-3175
www.onboardacademics.com
ISBN: 978-1-63096-038-4

OnBoard Academic's books are specifically designed to be used as printed workbooks or as on-screen instruction. Each page offers focused exercises and students quickly master topics with enough proficiency to move on to the next level.

OnBoard Academic's lessons are used in over 25,000 classrooms to rave reviews. Our lessons are aligned to the most recent governmental standards and are updated from time to time as standards change. Correlation documents are located on our website. Our lessons are created, edited and evaluated by educators to ensure top quality and real life success.

Interactive lessons for digital whiteboards, mobile devices, and PCs are available at www.onboardacademics.com. These interactive lessons make great additions to our books.

You can always reach us at customerservice@onboardacademics.com.

Complete Sentences

Key Vocabulary

sentence

subject

predicate

fragment

run-on sentence

A **sentence** is a group of words that forms a complete thought. It contains a **subject**, who or what the sentence is about, and a **predicate**, the action part of the sentence.

Read the sentences below. If the sentence is a complete sentence put a check mark in the box. If the sentence is incomplete put an X in the box.

Grace went to the store. ☐

Buying apples and oranges. ☐

Cans of tuna. ☐

Ice cream was on sale. ☐

The **subject** tells *who* or *what* the sentence is about.

Who

Jenna played checkers with me.

What

The car started to shake.

Identify the subject in each sentence and write it in the box.

	Owen visited the beach.
	His umbrella blew over.
	He brought a beach ball.
	The sand was hot.

The **predicate** is the action part of the sentence and describes the subject, or describes what the subject is doing.

describes the subject

David **has brown hair.**

describes what the subject is doing or has done.

The pitcher **threw a shutout.**

Identify the predicate
Underline the predicate in each sentence.

A large plane was flying over the ocean.

The pilot calmly operated the controls.

The seat was a little small for one large passenger.

Planes carry people from place to place.

Identify Complete Sentences

Indicate if the sentence is complete by placing a c in the box.
If the sentence is a fragment, indicate what is missing by placing an s in the box for a missing subject and a p in the box for a missing predicate.

A fragment is an incomplete sentence that is missing a *subject* or a *predicate*.

☐ Going to the zoo.

☐ The animals.

☐ The lions roared.

☐ Munched on bamboo sticks.

☐ The hyenas cackled.

☐ All of the students.

Ⓒ

Ⓟ

Ⓢ

Run-on Sentences.

If a sentence contains *multiple subjects and predicates*, it is called a run-on sentence and should be broken into two sentences.

For each of the sentences below make two separate sentences. Capitalize a word when necessary and add a period when necessary.

Grace went to the store Owen went to the beach.

Mia likes dogs she has a beagle.

The basketball team won the game they celebrated.

Jason had movie tickets someone gave them to him.

James did the dishes Brian dried them.

www.onboardacademics.com

Connect a blue subject with a green predicate to make the perfect sentence.

The blue water	**fly in the air.**
A lot of kids	**is perfect for swimming.**
Fish	**play at the beach.**
A hot day	**is cool and refreshing.**
Birds	**live in the ocean.**

Name_____

Complete Sentences Quiz

1. The predicate tells who or what the sentence is about. True or false?

2. Place a check mark next to the sentence with a missing predicate.
   a. I did my homework before dinner.
   b. The door slammed.
   c. The delicious chocolate pudding.
   d. She went shopping.

3. Place a check mark next to the complete sentence.
   a. All the kids at the beach.
   b. Played a game.
   c. Owen build a sandcastle.
   d. The beach ball.

4. Circle the word after which there should be a punctuation mark. We built a snowman it was four feet tall.

5. Circle the word after which there should be a punctuation mark. We drank hot cocoa with marshmallows it warmed us up.

Four Types of Sentences

Key Vocabulary

declarative sentence

exclamatory sentence

imperative sentence

interrogative sentence

Choose the most appropriate punctation mark to complete the sentence.

I have black hair ☐

That song is awesome ☐

Get in your basket, Rover ☐ or ☐

Did you get my email ☐

? **.** **!**

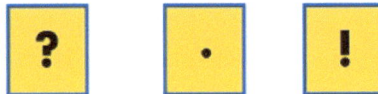

Declarative, exclamatory, imperative, and interrogative sentence.

I have black hair.
A *declarative sentence* makes a statement and ends with a period.

That song was awesome!
An *exclamatory sentence* shows a strong emotion and ends with an exclamation point.

Get in your basket, Rover.
An *imperative sentence* gives a command and ends with a period or an exclamation point.

Did you get my email?
An *interrogative sentence* asks a question and ends with a question mark.

Is the sentence imperative (IM), interrogative (IN), declarative (D), or exclamatory (E)?

That's so unfair!

What time is it?

My best friend's name is Tom.

Turn the TV down!

IM **IN** **D** **E**

An *imperative sentence* gives a command and ends with a period or an exclamation point.

An *interrogative sentence* asks a question and ends with a question mark.

A *declarative sentence* makes a statement and ends with a period.

An *exclamatory sentence* shows a strong emotion and ends with an exclamation point.

Which of these sentences are declarative?

I will call you tonight.	
Don't call me after 8 PM.	
What time will you call me?	
I'll be home if you call me at 8.	
That's much too late to call!	✓

Which of these sentences are imperative?

Can I borrow your ruler?	
Please pass me the ruler.	
I haven't got a ruler.	
Give me back my ruler!	
Hey, that's my ruler!	✓

Is the sentence imperative (IM), interrogative (IN), declarative (D) or exclamatory (E)?

Please also add the appropriate punctuation.

Okay every body it's time for today's grammar quiz

Please put your books away and take out your pencils

Does everyone understand the directions

Good luck everybody

IM　**IN**　**D**　**E**

Four Types of Sentences Quiz

1. An interrogative sentence usually ends with an exclamation point. True or false?

2. What type of sentence is the: I am going to the moves tonight.
   a. declarative
   b. imperative
   c. interrogative
   d. exclamatory

3. What type of sentence asks a question?
   a. declarative
   b. imperative
   c. interrogative
   d. exclamatory

4. What type of sentence gives a command?
   a. declarative
   b. imperative
   c. interrogative
   d. exclamatory

5. Which type of sentence is this: My dog is a golden retriever.
   a. declarative
   b. imperative
   c. interrogative
   d. exclamatory

Compound Sentences

Key Vocabulary

compound sentence

independent clause

coordinating conjunctions

Compound Sentences

A skillful surgeon performed the operation.

The patient made a full recovery.

———————

A skillful surgeon performed the operation, and the patient made a full recovery.

A compound sentence contains two or more independent clauses joined together with a coordinating conjunction.

Coordinating Conjunction

> # A coordinating conjunction connects words, phrases, or clauses of equal status.

Recall the acronym FANBOYS to remember the seven coordinating conjunctions.
Write a compound sentence using 4 of the coordinating conjunctions.

F	for
A	and
N	nor
B	but
O	or
Y	yet
S	so

Use these coordinating conjunctions to complete these compound sentences.

Tori went to see *The Blob*, ⬜ James recommended it.

Her mom said she could take a friend, ⬜ she took Mia.

They shared some popcorn, ⬜ they also split a drink.

Tori doesn't like salt on her popcorn, ⬜ does she like butter.

The movie had been out for 6 weeks, ⬜ the theater was busy.

"We can sit here," said Tori, " ⬜ we can sit at the back".

The Blob was dull, ⬜ the special effects were good.

| but | yet | so | for | and | or | nor |

Use coordinating conjunctions to join independent clauses in order to form three compound sentences.

for
and
nor
but
or
yet
so
,

I'd never eaten Indian food before. I ordered vindaloo.

The waiter said that vindaloo is very hot.

I really liked it a lot!   I ordered chicken korma.

We ate at an Indian restaurant last week.

Is this a compound sentence?

■ **subject**
■ **verb**

Joe plays the bass guitar, but can't sing.

No. Every sentence with a coordinating conjunction *is not* a compound sentence. A compound sentence also has to contain two or more independent clauses, and each independent clause has to have a subject and a verb. How could you make this a compound sentence?

Add another subject: Joe plays the bass guitar, but he can't sing.

√ **if the sentence is compound and X if it is not compound.**

1   James like pepperoni on his pizza but not anchovies. ☐

2   Allison is quite small yet she is the best player on her basketball team. ☐

3   I picked up a juicy apple and took a big bite. ☐

4   The left over chicken casserole was a day old but still tasted great! ☐

5   The telephone rang so I answered it. ☐

Name_____

Compound Sentences Quiz

1. All sentences with coordinating conjunctions are compound sentences. True or false?

2. Candice does not like rain, _____ does she like snow.
   a. for
   b. and
   c. nor
   d. but

3. The museum was huge, _____ we needed a guide map to find our way.

4. What are the coordinating conjunctions
   a. for, and, nor, but, or, yet, so
   b. from, an, not, because, of, yes, such
   c. if, when, while, where, although, then
   d. on, by near, to, over, across, under

5. The first two chapters were confusing, _____ the rest of the book was easy to understand.
   a. but
   b. for
   c. nor
   d. yet

Prepositional Phrases

Key Vocabulary

preposition

prepositional phrases

object of the preposition

www.onboardacademics.com

Prepositions and Prepositional Phrases

on   under   by

on the table   under the table   by the table

_____

Object of the Preposition

Prepositions specify things like direction, location and time. Prepositional phrases tell us about the *object* of the preposition: either a noun or a pronoun.

Fernando is waiting at the bus stop. He is waiting with me.

■ preposition
■ object of the preposition

Identify the prepositional phrases.

Write the prepositional phrases next to the corresponding number.

I used to live at 100 Center Street.

1

Owen was gone for two weeks.

2

I am taking the papers with me.

3

The class talked excitedly about the field trip.

4

We were waiting a long time at the bus stop.

5

Prepositions and Prepositional Objects

Underline the prepositions and circle the objects.

Mia has just arrived at school. She has to take a test after lunch, but has left her notes on the kitchen table. Her house is 3 miles from the school, so she is in a total panic. Fortunately, Mia's neighbor, Tori Jones, came to school by car. Maybe she can go back with Tori's Mom? Mrs. Jones tells Mia to get inside the car. She says they can be home and back in less than 30 minutes. Mia thanks Mrs. Jones for her kindness.

The Function of Prepositions

When a preposition modifies a noun or a pronoun, it acts an *adjective*.

The woman at the check-in desk was friendly.

noun   verb
preposition
object of preposition

When a preposition modifies a verb, it acts as an *adverb*.

She looked for the best possible seats.

Decide if the preposition acts like an adjective, adverb or neither.
Label the boxes accordingly.

① Jenna studies the menu with care. ☐

② The prices of the lunches are quite high. ☐

③ The server comes to her table. ☐

④ He asks if she is ready to order. ☐

⑤ She orders salad with blue cheese dressing. ☐

⑥ The server takes her order to the kitchen. ☐

ADJ Adjective   **ADV** Adverb   🚫 No preposition

Name_____

Prepositional Phrases Quiz

1. The object of a preposition can be a noun, a pronoun, or a verb. True or false?

2. Circle the preposition: The mouse scurried inside its hole.

3. Circle the prepositional phrase: She went to buy a gift at the mall.

4. Name the function of the preposition: Jamie chopped the vegetables on the cutting board.
   a. adjective
   b. adverb
   c. there is no preposition

5. What is the function of the preposition: Pablo finished the race before stopping for a drink.

6. How far are we _____ the resort?
   a. at
   b. from
   c. to
   d. before

Conjunctions

Key Vocabulary

conjunction

coordinating conjunction

subordinating (subordinate) conjunction

compound sentence

independent clause

Conjunctions

Instructions for the School Hiking Trip

Bring lunch `and` a snack.

Wear a sweatshirt `or` a light jacket.

We recommend old sneakers `but` not sandals.

There are bears, `so` keep to the trail!

WARNING!

Conjunctions link words, phrases, or clauses. The most commonly used conjunctions are and, but and or.

Conjunctions

Add conjunctions to this passage.

Hippos may look very friendly, [ ] they're not. Hippos [ ] Cape Buffalo are the two most dangerous large animals in all of Africa. Neither lions [ ] crocodiles cause as many human deaths. Hippos with young are especially dangerous, [ ] should be avoided at all times. Many people know about the dangers, [ ] still get too close to hippos and their young. Keep well back, [ ] you might regret it.

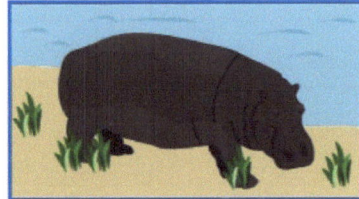

| nor | yet | and | so | or | but |

Coordinating Conjunctions

F for

A and

N nor

B but

O or

Y yet

S so

Conjunctions are used as 'joiners', and coordinating conjunctions are used to join two equal parts together, e.g. Dad likes coffee and tea. The FANBOYS acronym may help you to remember the coordinating conjunctions.

Coordinating Conjunctions and Compound Sentences

Matteus is a good student. His penmanship is poor.

Coordinating conjunctions are used to join two equal parts together. When the equal parts are sentences, the new sentence is called a **compound sentence.** The two parts of the compound sentence are called **independent clauses.**

Matteus

Matteus is a good student, but his penmanship is poor.

When a conjunction joins two independent clauses, it usually needs a comma.

Use coordinating conjunctions and rewrite the sentences as compound sentences.

Mia's Dad likes to play golf.
He is not very good at it.

Do you want pizza?
Would you rather have a sub?

Tori was bored.
She read a book.

Alison's mom is a teacher.
Owen's mom is an attorney.

Subordinating Conjunctions

The doctor examined the x-rays.
He concluded that Mia's leg was broken.

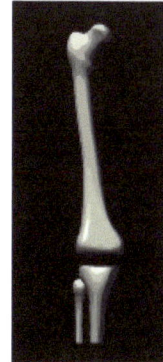

Subordinating conjunctions are used to connect **dependent clauses**: when one thing happens as a result of another.

When the doctor examined the x-rays,
he concluded that Mia's leg was broken.

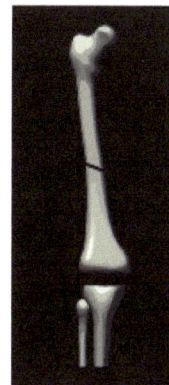

Commas

My allowance was increased **because** I made honor roll.

Because I made honor roll, my allowance was increased.

www.onboardacademics.com

Fill in the blanks with subordinating conjunctions.

[_____] we put on our costumes, my sister and I went trick or treating. [_____] we got home, we counted up our treats. We had collected over 50 pieces of candy, [_____] some of it was out of date. I took off my mask, [_____] I wouldn't scare my baby brother. [_____] he is only 2, he doesn't really understand Halloween. [_____] we are new to the neighborhood, my parents wanted to inspect the candy. They said we shouldn't eat the cookies, [_____] we know the family. Sadly, some cookies had to go in the trash, [_____] they looked delicious!

even though	unless	so that	although
Since	Because	When	After

Name_____

Conjunctions Quiz

1. Because is a coordinating conjunction. True or false?

2. Which of these conjunctions is not a subordinating conjunction?
   a. although
   b. since
   c. or
   d. when

3. He did not complete his chores, _____ did he finish his homework.

4. I finished my homework on time, _____ I was able to play with my friends.

5. _____ my brother woke up late, we were late for school.
   a. After
   b. Unless
   c. Although
   d. Because

6. If a comma is needed, add it. Because I was full I skipped dessert.

www.ingramcontent.com/pod-product-compliance
Lightning Source LLC
Chambersburg PA
CBHW042020080426

42735CB00002B/112